P9-CEV-955

Alaska

BY ANN HEINRICHS

Content Adviser: Candace Waugaman, President, Alaska Historical Society Board, Fairbanks, Alaska

Reading Adviser: Dr. Linda D. Labbo, Department of Reading Education, College of Education, The University of Georgia

COMPASS POINT BOOKS ✦ MINNEAPOLIS, MINNESOTA

Compass Point Books
3109 West 50th Street, #115
Minneapolis, MN 55410

Visit Compass Point Books on the Internet at *www.compasspointbooks.com*
or e-mail your request to *custserv@compasspointbooks.com*

On the cover: Caribou and the north side of Mount McKinley in Denali National Park

Photographs ©: 2002 Calvin Hall/AlaskaStock.com, cover, 1; Jeff Greenberg/Visuals Unlimited, 3, 36;
Photo Network/Mark Newman, 4; Digital Vision, 6, 45; Science VU/NASA/Visuals Unlimited, 8; Unicorn
Stock Photos/Jeff Greenberg, 9, 27, 42; Patrick J. Endres/Visuals Unlimited, 10; Joe McDonald/
Tom Stack & Associates, 11; Richard Hamilton Smith, 12; Hugh Rose/Visuals Unlimited, 13; North Wind
Picture Archives, 14, 17; Hulton/Archive by Getty Images, 15, 16, 18, 41, 46; Thomas Kitchin/Tom
Stack & Associates, 19, 34; Ernest Manewal/Visuals Unlimited, 20; McCutcheon/Visuals Unlimited, 21,
26, 33, 44 (middle); Courtesy of the Office of the Governor, State of Alaska, 23; Corbis/Carl Purcell, 24;
Corbis/Danny Lehman, 25; U.S. Department of Agriculture/Ron Nichols, 28, 47; John Elk III, 29, 48
(top); Corbis/Galen Rowell, 30; Photo Network/Bachman, 31; Mark Newman/Tom Stack & Associates,
32; Photo Network/Nancy Hoyt Belcher, 35; Photo Network/Belcher, 39; Robert McCaw, 40, 43 (top);
Robesus, Inc., 43 (state flag); One Mile Up, Inc., 43 (state seal); Unicorn Stock Photos/R.E. Barber, 44
(top); Artville, 44 (bottom).

Editors: E. Russell Primm, Emily J. Dolbear, and Patricia Stockland
Photo Researcher: Marcie C. Spence
Photo Selector: Linda S. Koutris
Designer/Page Production: The Design Lab/Jaime Martens
Cartographer: XNR Productions, Inc.

Library of Congress Cataloging-in-Publication Data
Heinrichs, Ann.
  Alaska / by Ann Heinrichs.
    p. cm.— (This land is your land)
  Includes bibliographical references and index.
  Contents: Welcome to Alaska!—Mountains, glaciers, and tundra—A trip through time—
Government by the people—Alaskans at work—Getting to know Alaskans—Let's explore Alaska!
  ISBN 0-7565-0337-X
  1. Alaska—Juvenile literature. [1. Alaska.] I. Title. II. Series: Heinrichs, Ann. This land is your land.
F904.3.H448 2003
979.8—dc   212002012861

© 2004 by Compass Point Books
All rights reserved. No part of this book may be reproduced without written permission from the
publisher. The publisher takes no responsibility for the use of any of the materials or methods described
in this book, nor for the products thereof.
Printed in the United States of America.

Table of Contents

NOTE: In this book, words that are defined in the glossary are in **bold** the first time they appear in the text.

▲ Alaska's rugged wilderness can be seen in Denali National Park.

. . . We always knew / We could walk the wind / And it would carry us / Back home.

Fred Bigjim wrote this poem. He is an **Alaskan Native** of the Inupiat group. Fred grew up in the icy **Arctic** region. As a child, he walked the windswept land without fear. He knew that ravens and foxes watched and protected him.

Alaska's Natives lived in harmony with their land. For newcomers, though, Alaska was a challenge. There were mountains to cross and frozen soil to conquer. Settlers lived in fear of grizzly bears and wolves.

Alaska, the largest state, is called the Last **Frontier.** It was America's last unexplored wilderness. Even today, much of Alaska remains wild. Towering mountains rise over the rugged landscape. Wild animals roam free.

In the 1890s, Alaska was famous for its gold. Today, it's one of the country's largest oil producers. Still, Alaskans believe in protecting their land. Alaska's Aleut people named Alaska the Great Land. Now you'll see what a great land it is!

Mountains, Glaciers, and Tundra

▲ Along with the largest glaciers, Alaska has the tallest mountains in the United States.

Do you like to play baseball? Imagine playing a midnight base-ball game—in broad daylight! For many Alaskans, midnight fun is a normal activity. Alaska is called the Land of the Midnight Sun. It's so far north that the summer sun stays out for long hours. Winter can be a gloomy time, though. Daylight hours are short. Northern Alaska can be pitch-dark at noon!

Alaska is the largest state in the country. It's more than twice the size of Texas, the next-largest state. Alaska has thousands of islands and peninsulas. It's not joined to the rest of the United States. Alaskans call the forty-eight connected states the Lower 48. America's tallest mountains and biggest glaciers are in Alaska. Glaciers are massive chunks of ice. They look like mountains—and people climb them, too.

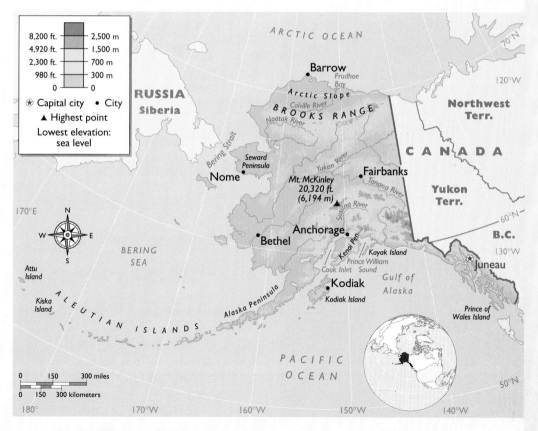

▲ **A topographic map of Alaska**

Canada runs along Alaska's eastern border and part of its southern border. Water surrounds the state on all other sides. To the north is the Arctic Ocean. To the south is the Pacific Ocean. The Bering Sea lies to the west. The narrow Bering Strait is only about 50 miles (80 kilometers) wide. On the other side is Siberia, a part of Russia and northern Kazakhstan.

Alaska has two long "tails." Both are formed by high mountain ranges. On the southwest are the Alaska Peninsula and the Aleutian Islands. On the southeast is Alaska's Panhandle. Juneau, the state capital, is the major city

▲ The Bering Strait lies to the west of Alaska.

▲ **From this dock in Juneau, you can see mountains behind the city.**

there. Anchorage, Alaska's largest city, is on Cook Inlet near

the southern coast of central Alaska. To the south are the

Kenai Peninsula and Kodiak Island.

▲ **Mount McKinley in Denali National Park is the highest peak in North America.**

Travel north from Anchorage, and you enter Alaska's vast Interior. Its crowning point is Mount McKinley, North America's highest peak. It is located in Denali National Park. The Yukon River—Alaska's longest river—cuts across the Interior. Fairbanks is the region's largest city. Much of the Interior is known as the bush. That means land that cannot be reached by roads.

Northern Alaska is the Arctic region. The area north of the Brooks Range is called the Arctic Slope. Part of it is protected as the Arctic National Wildlife Refuge. Point Barrow is Alaska's northernmost point.

Land in the Arctic region is called tundra. It's cold and dry, like a frozen desert. Trees cannot grow there, but mosses, grasses, and tough little shrubs do. In the springtime, the tundra is ablaze with flowering plants.

▲ Grasses and other plants create beautiful fall colors in Denali National Park.

Herds of caribou migrate across the tundra. They are a type of large deer that live in Arctic regions. Elk and deer live in parts of southern Alaska. Reindeer, moose, polar bears, and grizzly bears also live in Alaska. Seals, walrus, and sea otters swim near the coast. Whales leap in the coastal waters.

Alaska has strict laws to protect its wildlife. Sometimes, though, pollution and human mistakes cause disasters. In 1989, the oil ship *Exxon Valdez* crashed in Prince William Sound, not far from Anchorage. It spilled millions of gallons of oil. Thousands of fish and seabirds were killed.

▲ **A moose grazes in Denali National Park.**

▲ **Northern lights create bright colors in the night sky over the Brooks Range.**

Every winter, Alaskans watch the **aurora borealis,** or northern lights. These flashes of light dance across the night sky. They're a dazzling range of colors, from red and green to purple.

Many of Alaska's southern mountains are volcanoes. Some are not active, but others pour out smoke constantly. Alaskans also watch out for earthquakes. An earthquake struck the Anchorage area in 1964. It was North America's worst earthquake ever.

Alaska gets all kinds of weather. Snow blankets the land in the winter. Parts of the Panhandle, Alaska's southeastern coast and a series of surrounding islands, are often rainy and foggy. The Interior gets warm summers and cold winters. As you can guess, the Arctic region is cold and dry.

▲ **Alaskan Natives hunting deer in the snow**

People have lived in Alaska for thousands of years. The first

major groups were Inuit, Aleut, and American Indian people.

The Inuit occupied the Arctic coastal regions. They hunted

fish, whales, seals, caribou, and polar bears. Aleuts lived on the Aleutian Islands and the Alaska Peninsula. Tlingit, Haida, and Tsimshian people were Native American groups. They lived along the southeast coast.

Russian explorers were the first Europeans in Alaska. Russia sent Vitus Bering on two voyages, in 1728 and 1741. He landed on Kayak Island and claimed this land for Russia. More Russians arrived to hunt sea otters, beavers, and seals for their furs. They battled the Tlingit and other Native peoples for their land. Grigory Shelikhov set up a fur-trading post on Kodiak Island in 1784. Aleksandr Baranov set up the town of New Archangel in 1799. The name was changed to Sitka when the United States purchased this land many years later.

▲ Aleksandr Baranov was the first governor of Russian America.

▲ William Seward was responsible for buying Alaska for the United States.

Meanwhile, Americans wanted to fish and mine in Alaska. Secretary of State William Seward suggested buying Alaska. People laughed at him. They thought Alaska was nothing but ice. They called it Seward's Icebox and Seward's Folly. Despite this, in 1867, the United States bought Alaska for $7.2 million.

The purchase turned out to be a great idea. Joseph Juneau and Richard Harris discovered gold in Alaska in 1880. The nearby town was first named Harrisburg, but by 1881, the name was changed to Juneau. More gold was found in Nome and the Klondike region of Yukon Territory. The gold rush was on! Thousands of miners rushed in to strike it rich.

Alaska became a U.S. territory in 1912. By that time, Alaska had busy coal and copper mines. Many factories were making canned salmon, too.

▲ The capital city was named after Joseph Juneau, who found gold in Alaska.

World War II (1939–1945) was a tense time for Alaskans. Japan bombed U.S. ships at Pearl Harbor, Hawaii, in 1941. At once, the United States declared war on Japan. The army built the Alaska Highway as a military supply road. Alaska was important because Japan lay very close to the Aleutian Islands. In 1942, Japan captured Attu and Kiska Islands. American troops won them back the next year. This was the war's only action on American soil.

Alaska became the forty-ninth U.S. state in 1959. The new state soon had a treasure even more valuable than gold.

▲ **Soldiers with frostbitten feet on Attu Island during World War II**

▲ The Trans-Alaskan pipeline winds through the wilderness.

It was "black gold"! That means petroleum, or oil. It was discovered on Prudhoe Bay in 1968. This turned out to be the biggest oil field in the United States. The Trans-Alaskan Pipeline opened in 1977. It carried oil to the port of Valdez. Taxes on oil brought millions of dollars to the state. Meanwhile, Alaska's Native peoples fought for their land rights. They won back millions of acres of land in 1971.

Today, the whole country argues over Alaska's Arctic National Wildlife Refuge. Some people want to drill for oil there. Others want to protect the land. The state works hard to balance everyone's needs.

No one's too young to take part in government. Just look at Alaska's schoolchildren. Alaska held a contest for students in 1926. The contest was to draw a design for Alaska's flag. Thirteen-year-old Benny Benson won. Benny's design is Alaska's state flag today.

Children got involved again in 1992. More than eleven thousand students voted for a state insect. The four-spot skimmer dragonfly won. The students then wrote to their state senator. She introduced the dragonfly **bill** in 1995—and it passed!

▲ **The Alaska state flag hangs under the United States flag.**

▲ The state capitol in Juneau, where the legislature makes state laws

Alaska's state government works just like the U.S. government. It has three branches—legislative, executive, and judicial. The legislative branch makes the state laws. Voters choose their lawmakers to serve in Alaska's legislature. The legislature has two houses, or sections. One is the twenty-member senate. The other is the forty-member house of representatives. Both houses must approve new laws. That includes the laws that created the state flag and state insect.

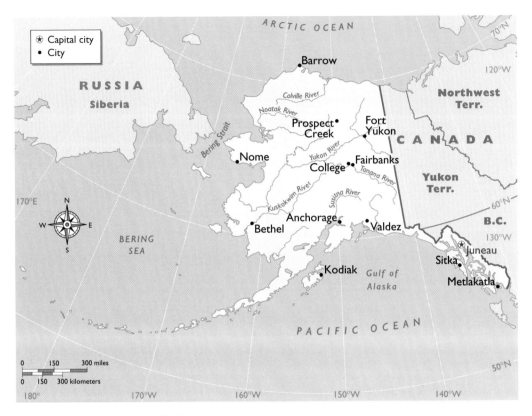

▲ **A geopolitical map of Alaska**

The executive branch makes sure the laws are carried out. Alaska's governor is the head of the executive branch. Alaskans choose a governor every four years. The governor can serve only two terms in a row. Governors appoint commissioners to run various departments. The legislature must approve the commissioners.

Alaska's judges and courts make up the judicial branch.

They decide whether laws have been broken. The highest court is Alaska's state supreme court. It consists of five judges. The governor appoints them.

▲ **Governor Frank H. Murkowski**

▲ The city government in Skagway meets in city hall.

Most states are divided into counties. Alaska is different. It has sixteen "organized boroughs." A large portion of the state is still unorganized, however, without any borough government. These areas have too few people. Boroughs are governed by a mayor or manager and an **assembly.** Most cities also have mayors or managers, plus city councils.

In the 1890s, mining in Alaska meant mining gold. Today, Alaska ranks fourth among gold-producing states. Oil brings in almost all the state's mining income. Alaska is the nation's second-biggest oil producer, after Texas. Oil is found on the Kenai Peninsula, Cook Inlet, and Prudhoe Bay. Wherever oil is found, there is usually natural gas, too.

▲ **This oil platform is located in Cook Inlet, near Anchorage.**

Alaska's mines produce other minerals, too. In 2000, Alaska ranked first among the states in zinc. It was second in lead and silver. Other valuable minerals are coal, platinum, tin, and molybdenum.

▲ A potato field near Anchorage

The Matanuska Valley is Alaska's richest farming region. The Susitna and Tanana River valleys are fertile, too. Decorative flowers and trees are the most valuable farm products. Potatoes, cabbage, cauliflower, and barley are the major crops. The long hours of sunlight sometimes produce giant-sized vegetables even though the temperatures never get very high. Along with plants, some farmers raise beef cattle, milk cows, and pigs.

Alaska is the country's top state for fish. Fishers bring in salmon, herring, and halibut. They catch shrimp and crabs, too. Alaska's Natives raise reindeer for their meat and hides. Some also trap animals for their furs.

Most of Alaska's factories process local goods. For example, oil is made into gasoline and chemicals. Some factories make milk products and packaged meat. Fish are canned or frozen.

▲ A commercial fishing harbor in Hoonah

Service workers in Alaska hold many types of jobs. They may work in restaurants or rent airplanes. Some are computer programmers, teachers, or health care workers. Alaska has many government workers, too. They may work in national parks, military bases, or social service offices.

▲ Service workers near Homer collect information about plants for the government.

▲ **Many Alaskans fly planes instead of driving cars. These planes are located in Anchorage.**

How would you like to fly to the grocery store? If you lived in Alaska, you might have to! It can be hard to get around in Alaska. Much of the state can be reached only by air. Thousands of Alaskans have bush planes instead of cars. They fly their food and other supplies home. Juneau, the capital, can be reached only by water or air.

In 2000, there were 626,932 people in Alaska. Only Vermont and Wyoming have fewer people. No other state has people spread about so thinly. Suppose all Alaskans were spread out evenly across the state. They would occupy almost 1 square mile (2.6 sq km) apiece! Most residents actually live in city areas. Anchorage and Fairbanks are two of the largest cities. Two out of five Alaskans live in Anchorage. Fairbanks is a center for business and travel in the Interior.

About seven out of ten Alaskans are white. The next-largest group are Alaska's Natives. They make up almost one out of six residents. Asians, African-Americans, Pacific Islanders, and **Hispanics** live in Alaska, too.

▲ Some Alaskans live in isolated wilderness areas.

▲ Commercial fishermen aboard a boat in Valdez

The Inuit, or Eskimos, are the largest Native group. Most live along the coasts of the Arctic Ocean and Bering Sea. They fish, hunt, and trap fur-bearing animals. Some raise herds of reindeer. The Aleut are closely related to the Inuit. They live in the Aleutian Islands and other southern areas.

American Indians are the second-largest Native group. They include the Tlingit, Haida, Tsimshian, and Athabascan. The Tlingit have many traditional crafts. They include wood carving and blanket weaving. The Haida and Tsimshian live along the Panhandle. Many Tsimshian people live in the village of Metlakatla. Most of Alaska's Haida people live on Prince of Wales Island. Both groups carve beautiful totem poles. They show traditional spirit figures such as eagles or bears. The Athabascan are scattered around the Interior.

Alaska's most famous event is the Iditarod. (It's pronounced *eye-DIT-a-rod.*) It's an exciting **dog-mushing,** or sled-dog, race.

▲ **Racing sled dogs can be an exciting event.**

Mushers race from Anchorage to Nome. It can take three weeks to finish! Many other towns hold dog-mushing races.

The Anchorage Fur Rendezvous is in February. It's a weeklong festival of fur sales, dog-mushing, and games. Fairbanks holds an ice-sculpture contest every March. Alaska Day in Sitka celebrates the 1867 Alaska Purchase.

The longest day of sunlight is in June. That's when many cities hold Midnight Sun festivals. Nome has its Polar Bear Swim then, too. People plunge into the icy water for a teeth-chattering swim.

▲ **One entry from the ice-sculpture contest in Fairbanks**

▲ Cruise ships are a common sight along Alaska's Panhandle.

There are two ways to tour Alaska's Panhandle—boat and boat! Some "boats" are ferries traveling the Marine Highway. Other "boats" are ships that cruise the **Inside Passage.** This waterway runs past islands, glaciers, and towering rock walls.

Near Ketchikan is Saxman Indian Village. It has the world's largest collection of totem poles. Sitka was once Alaska's Russian capital. Saint Michael's Cathedral still stands from Russian times. Like other Russian Orthodox churches, it has an onion-shaped dome. Inside are icons, or paintings of religious figures.

▲ **The Totem Park at Saxman Indian Village**

▲ **People look small compared to the Mendenhall Glacier.**

In Juneau, you can tour the state capitol. The Alaska State Museum is in Juneau, too. From Auk Bay near Juneau, you can take hiking trails up Mendenhall Glacier. You'll feel tiny in the deep inlets of Glacier Bay. You'll pass towering glaciers, icebergs, and cliffs. Farther north is Malaspina, Alaska's largest glacier.

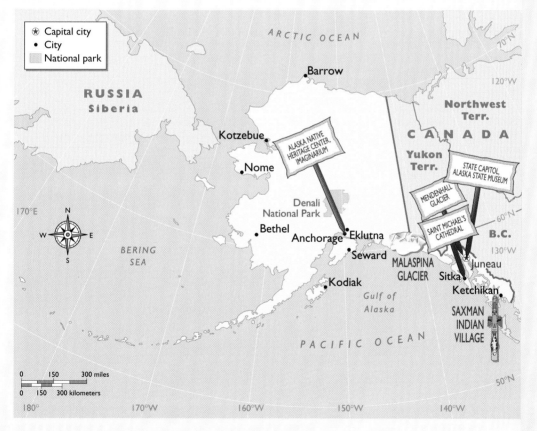

▲ **Places to visit in Alaska**

The Alaska Native Heritage Center is in Anchorage. It has villages of eleven Native groups. Native guides explain their culture. The Imaginarium is a hands-on science museum. There you'll learn all about the northern lights, glaciers, polar bears, and much more. From Anchorage, you can go to the Kenai Peninsula. You can take hiking trails into the mountains, or watch bears catch salmon in the streams. From Seward, you can take a boat trip along the Kenai **Fjords.**

Mount McKinley in Denali National Park is the highest point of the Interior of Alaska—and the highest point in North America. You can hike or take a bus through the park. You'll pass many glaciers along the way. You'll also see moose, caribou, and grizzly bears.

Fairbanks is known as a great place to watch the northern lights. It's also the northern end of good highways. Most travelers in Alaska only go this far. However, you can take air trips farther north or travel by dirt road to the Yukon River or the Arctic Ocean.

▲ **An inn along Main Street of Nome**

Nome is a coastal town on the Seward Peninsula. Seals and walrus flop up onto the icy banks. Most residents of Kotzebue are Inupiat people. They're a branch of the Inuit. They hang their whale and fish catches on drying racks.

Vast stretches of Arctic tundra cover northern Alaska. Herds of caribou pass by, nibbling on tundra plants. Barrow is as far north as you can go. Stand on Point Barrow and look north. What lies beyond? Though you cannot see it, the North Pole is straight ahead. Behind you lies the majestic wilderness of Alaska—truly a Great Land!

▲ Caribou are just one of the many natural attractions that make Alaska an amazing place to visit.

Important Dates

1741   Vitus Bering and Aleksey Chirikov are the first Europeans to see Alaska; Bering claims Alaska for Russia.

1784   Grigory Shelikhov establishes a settlement at Three Saints Bay on Kodiak Island.

1867   The United States buys Alaska from Russia for $7.2 million.

1880   Joseph Juneau discovers gold near present-day Juneau; Alaska's gold rush begins.

1896   Gold is discovered in the Klondike region.

1899   Gold is discovered in Nome.

1912   Alaska becomes a U.S. territory.

1942   In World War II, Japan attacks the Aleutian Islands; the Alaska Highway is built.

1959   Alaska becomes the forty-ninth U.S. state on January 3.

1968   America's largest oil field is discovered on Prudhoe Bay.

1971   The Alaska Native Claims Settlement Act returns land to Alaska's Native people.

1973   The first Iditarod sled-dog race is held.

1977   The Trans-Alaskan Pipeline opens.

1989   The tanker *Exxon Valdez* spills millions of gallons of oil in Prince William Sound.

2001   The Special Olympics World Winter Games are held in Anchorage, drawing more than 10,000 athletes, coaches, friends, and family; it is the largest event ever held in Alaska.

Glossary

Alaskan Native—the name given to the group of Alaskans who are originally from the area; they are also called Native peoples

Arctic—Earth's northernmost region; the area at and around the North Pole

assembly—a group of people meeting for a specific purpose

aurora borealis—lights appearing in the sky above Earth's northern regions; also called the northern lights

bill—a suggested law

dog-mushing—a race in which a team of dogs is used to pull a sled

fjords—deep, narrow waterways

frontier—an area that is not yet explored or settled

Hispanic—people of Mexican, South American, and other Spanish-speaking cultures

Inside Passage—a protected shipping route from Puget Sound, Washington, to Skagway, Alaska, that follows channels between the mainland and coastal islands

Did You Know?

★ Alaska has seventeen of America's twenty highest peaks.

★ Athabascan Indians gave Mount McKinley the name "Denali." It means "the Great One."

★ The word *Alaska* came from the Aleut word *alayeska* meaning "great land" or "mainland."

★ In Barrow, the sun never sets between May 10 and August 2. In the winter, the sun sets on November 18 and doesn't rise again until January 24.

★ Canadian Indians called the Inuit people Eskimos. That name means "eaters of raw meat." However, like other Alaskan Natives, the Inuit cure or cook their meat.

★ The U.S. government controls more than half of Alaska's land. Most of this land is national parks and wildlife refuges. America's six largest national parks are in Alaska.

★ Alaska's Yukon River is the nation's third-longest river. It's the fifth-longest river in North America.

State capital: Juneau

State motto: North to the Future

State nicknames: The Last Frontier, The Great Land, Land of the Midnight Sun

Statehood: January 3, 1959; forty-ninth state

Land area: 570,374 square miles (1,477,269 sq km); **rank:** first

Highest point: Mount McKinley, 20,320 feet (6,194 m)

Lowest point: Sea level along the coast

Highest recorded temperature: 100°F (38°C) at Fort Yukon on June 27, 1915

Lowest recorded temperature: −80°F (−62°C) at Prospect Creek on January 23, 1971

Average January temperature: 5°F (−13°C)

Average July temperature: 55°F (13°C)

Population in 2000: 626,932; **rank:** forty-eight

Largest cities in 2000: Anchorage (260,283), Juneau (30,711), Fairbanks (30,224)

Factory products: Petroleum products, food products

Farm products: Decorative plants, potatoes, barley, vegetables

Fishery products: Cod, crab, salmon, flounder

Mining products: Petroleum, gold, zinc

State flag: Alaska's state flag features eight gold stars on a field of blue. The blue field stands for the sky and for Alaska's  state flower, the forget-me-not. Seven stars form the shape of the Big Dipper. It's one of the constellations, or patterns of stars, in the night sky. The Big Dipper's Latin name is *Ursa Major,* or "big bear." It stands for Alaska's strength. The Big Dipper's "pointer stars" point to the North Star. It's the larger, brighter star in the upper right-hand corner. It stands for Alaska's future.

State seal: The state seal shows many symbols of Alaska's natural and economic wealth. In the background,  rays shine above the mountains. They stand for the northern lights. A smelter stands for mining. A train represents Alaska's railroads, and ships represent sea transportation. Trees symbolize Alaska's timber resources. A farmer, with his horse and bundles of wheat, stands for Alaska's agriculture. A fish shows the importance of fishing.

State abbreviation: AK (postal)

State Symbols

State bird: Willow ptarmigan

State flower: Forget-me-not

State tree: Sitka spruce

State fish: King salmon

State land mammal: Moose

State marine mammal: Bowhead whale

State insect: Four-spotted skimmer dragonfly

State mineral: Gold

State gem: Jade

State fossil: Woolly mammoth

State sport: Dog mushing

Making Baked Alaska

Baked Alaska was invented at a New York restaurant to celebrate the Alaska Purchase.

Makes eight servings.

INGREDIENTS:

1 cup raspberries, strawberries, or blueberries

2 quarts softened ice cream, vanilla or chocolate

4 egg whites

¼ teaspoon salt

½ cup sugar

DIRECTIONS:

Make sure an adult helps you with the hot stove. Take a pie plate or other deep dish that's 9 inches across. Spread the fruit in the bottom. Add the ice cream, spreading evenly. Chill in the freezer until it's firm. Meanwhile, preheat the oven to 450°F. Beat the egg whites until they're foamy. Slowly add the salt and sugar. Beat until the mixture is stiff and stands up in peaks. Remove the freezer mixture. Spread the egg whites on top. Place on the lowest oven shelf. Bake for about 8 minutes, or until the egg whites are lightly brown. Serve right away.

"Alaska's Flag"

Words by Marie Drake, music by Elinor Dusenbury

Eight stars of gold on a field of blue—
Alaska's flag. May it mean to you
The blue of the sea, the evening sky,
The mountain lakes, and the flow'rs nearby,
The gold of the early sourdough dreams,
The precious gold of the hills and streams;
The brilliant stars in the northern sky,
The *Bear*—the *Dipper*—and, shining high,
The great North Star with its steady light,
O'er land and sea a beacon bright.
Alaska's flag—to Alaskans dear,
The simple flag of a last frontier.

Aleksandr Baranov (1747–1819) was a Russian fur trader. Baranov (pictured above left) was the first governor of Russian America. In 1799, he founded New Archangel, or Sitka.

Vitus Bering (1681–1741) was an explorer from Denmark who sailed for Russia. Sailing through the strait that bears his name, Bering proved in 1728 that Asia and North America are separate continents. In 1741 he explored Alaska's coast. He died and is buried on Bering Island.

Susan Butcher (1954–) is a sled-dog racer. She was the first person to win three Iditarod races in a row—1986, 1987, and 1988. She won again in 1990. Butcher was born in Massachusetts.

Walter Joseph Hickel (1919–) was born in Kansas and moved to Alaska in 1940. He fought for Alaskan statehood, worked under President Nixon as secretary of the Interior, and served as governor of Alaska (1966–1969; 1990–1993).

Jewel (1974–) is a singer and actress. Her song "You Were Meant for Me" was a hit in 1996. Her album *Pieces of You* won several Grammy nominations in 1997. Her last name is Kilcher.

Joseph Juneau (1826?–1900) discovered gold near Juneau in 1880. This led to Alaska's gold rush.

Jack London (1876–1916) was an author. He lived in the Yukon in the 1890s. Based on his experiences there, he wrote *Call of the Wild* and *White Fang*. London was born in California.

Ray Mala (1906–1952) was an actor. He was half Jewish and half Inuit. Mala was sometimes called Mala the Magnificent. He starred in the series *Robinson Crusoe of Clipper Island* (1940) as well as other films. He was born Ray Wise.

Elizabeth Peratrovich (1911–1958) was a Tlingit woman who fought for Natives' rights. Through her efforts, Alaska passed its first antidiscrimination law in 1945.

Joe Redington Sr. (1917–1999) is called the Father of the Iditarod. He began managing the event in 1967. He was born in Oklahoma.

Libby Riddles (1956–) is a sled-dog racer. In 1985, she became the first woman to win the Iditarod. She was born in Wisconsin.

Grigory Shelikhov (1747–1795) was a Russian fur trader. He established Three Saints Bay on Kodiak Island in 1784.

Want to Know More?

At the Library

Brown, Tricia. *Children of the Midnight Sun.* Anchorage: Alaska Northwest Books, 1998.

Cobb, Vicki, and Barbara Lavallee (illustrator). *This Place Is Cold.* New York: Walker & Co., 1991.

Fowler, Susi Gregg, and Peter Catalanotto (illustrator). *Circle of Thanks.* New York: Scholastic Trade, 1998.

Italia, Bob. *Alaska.* Edina, Minn.: Abdo & Daughters, 1998.

Kimmel, Elizabeth Cody, and Nora Koerber (illustrator). *Balto and the Great Race.* New York: Random Library, 2000.

Morey, Walt, and John Schoenherr (illustrator). *Gentle Ben.* New York: Puffin, 1992.

Nichols, Richard. *A Story to Tell: Traditions of a Tlingit Community.* Minneapolis: Lerner, 1998.

Somervill, Barbara A. *Alaska.* Danbury, Conn.: Children's Press, 2002.

On the Web

State of Alaska Online
http://www.state.ak.us/
To learn about Alaska's history, government, economy, and land

Travel Alaska
http://www.travelalaska.com
To find out about Alaska's events, activities, and sights

Through the Mail

Alaska Division of Tourism
P.O. Box 110801
Juneau, AK 99811
For information on travel and interesting sights in Alaska

Alaska State Library
Historical Library
P.O. Box 110571
Juneau, AK 99811
For information on Alaska's history

On the Road

Alaska State Capitol
Fourth Street between Seward and Main
Juneau, Alaska 99801
907/465-3800
To visit Alaska's state capitol

About the Author

Ann Heinrichs grew up in Fort Smith, Arkansas, and lives in Chicago. She is the author of more than one hundred books for children and young adults on Asian, African, and U.S. history and culture. Ann has also written numerous newspaper, magazine, and encyclopedia articles. She is an award-winning martial artist, specializing in t'ai chi empty-hand and sword forms.

Ann has traveled widely throughout the United States, Africa, Asia, and the Middle East. In exploring each state for this series, she rediscovered the people, history, and resources that make this a great land, as well as the concerns we share with people around the world.